workplan

creative

new media

strategy

Ad Campaign Planner

Shay Sayre
Professor of Advertising
California State University
Fullerton, California

oadcast

promotion

internet

audience

public relations

agency

event planning

target

SOUTH-WESTERN College Publishing
An International Thomson Publishing Company

Publisher/Team Director: John Szilagyi
Acquisitions Editor: Dreis Van Landuyt
Developmental Editor: Judy O'Neill
Production Editor: Mardell Toomey
Production House: Rudd Publication Services
Marketing Manager: Sara Woelfel

Copyright © 1998
by SOUTH-WESTERN COLLEGE PUBLISHING
Cincinnati, Ohio
An International Thomson Publishing Company

ISBN: 0-538-87894-0

1 2 3 4 5 PN 3 2 1 0 9 8

Printed in the United States of America

I(T)P®
International Thomson Publishing
South-Western Publishing is an ITP Company.
The ITP trademark is used under license.

TABLE OF CONTENTS

INTRODUCTION

Using Your *Ad Campaign Planner*

This workbook is designed to take you through the various aspects of an advertising campaign, including the preparation of a plans book and client "pitch." You will work with a group of students in a simulated agency to develop an integrated communications program for one of the clients presented in this planner.

An integrated campaign consists of advertising, sales promotion, public relations, and direct selling activities that are focused on persuasive communications for a client. Clients can be consumer or business products manufacturers, nonprofit organizations, retailers, or companies.

The goal of a campaign is to reach a targeted market segment with a particular client message that results in achieving communication objectives such as creating or increasing awareness, changing or maintaining an attitude, and developing incentives to stimulate purchase intention.

This *Planner* contains Preliminary Planning Activities designed to supplement your advertising text and relate theory to the task of actual implementation. Simulating the real-life process that advertising agencies use to develop a campaign, these exercises will enable you to see how objectives translate into strategies, and how strategies are developed into usable tactics.

Eight Practicing Your Skills Exercises are included to help you understand particular concepts, along with two Outside Assignments to immerse you in the advertising industry.

Preparing an entire campaign in one semester is a formidable task requiring time, energy, and cooperation. During the process, you will experience the excitement and frustration involved in assembling the pieces of a unique puzzle that results in a full-blown campaign. For an example of a campaign produced by an introductory advertising class, turn to the Appendix.

You can expect that preparing this campaign will stimulate your creative juices and release your untapped ideas. Use this campaign to test your aptitude for this competitive and passionate business. And if you dare, send us your campaign so we can include it as an example in the next edition of the Planner.

The *Ad Campaign Planner* consists of seven parts:

In Part I, you will select a client from among the choices presented.

Part II helps you to direct your talents into a particular agency role, and to organize your agency.

Preliminary Planning Activities found in Part III correspond with the subject matter in your text; once completed, they form the foundation for agency decisions.

Agency and team meeting agendas appear in Parts IV and V.

The eight Practicing Your Skills Exercises presented in Part VI will provide you with an opportunity for hands-on practice with the concepts discussed in your text.

Part VII offers two Outside Activities: an informational interview with an advertising professional and a book report. Reading suggestions and report forms are included.

In addition, the Appendix contains an example of a student campaign plans book for NYNEX Cellular.

the *market*

Part I:
Selecting
a Client

product

price

problem

company

background

One of the two companies featured in this section will be your client. Manufacturers of hygiene and sneaker products were selected for the familiarity and accessibility of these products to college students. After reading each company's synopsis, select the product best suited to your interest and experience.

VANS FOOTWEAR

COMPANY BACKGROUND

Vans, Inc., is a California-based casual footwear manufacturer established in 1966 by Paul Van Doren to manufacture canvas shoes and sell them directly to the public through company-owned stores. Embraced by skateboarders in the 1970s and Motocross riders in the 1980s, Vans' popularity went nationwide when Jeff Spicoli wore a pair of black and white checked Vans in the movie *Fast Times at Ridgemont High*.

In 1988, the venture-banking firm of McCown DeLeeuw purchased Vans with the intention of expanding sales of the fashion-oriented shoes nationally and internationally. In 1991, the company went public and trades on NASDAQ. By 1994, Vans had about 2,500 employees and manufactured 4 million pairs of shoes annually. Sales were $43.7 million and sales to retailers increased 38%.

MARKET

Although the company characterizes its customers by attitude as "people who are confident enough to take a stand," traditional core Vans customers have been males, ages 12–17, and males and females who associate the brand with skateboarding. Women in the 18–40 age group who are considered trendsetters have become the second largest market segment for Vans.

MARKETING MIX

- *Product*

    Casual athletic footwear, Vans shoes are distinguished by their high-profile sole, wide variety of fabrics and colors, and the fact that custom patterns and sizes can be specially ordered. Vans claims that its product is more than a shoe; it's a "collection of benefits we provide to our customers." Vans' most popular collections include: Native, hip-hop, Crescent Island, cool basics, and the Authentic for men and women in slip-ons, decks, midcuts, and high-tops, and a line for kids. Fabrics include canvas, suede, velvet, denim, flannel, corduroy, linen, wool, and hemp.

- *Price*

  Vans prides itself on being affordable. With prices between $25 and $50, Vans shoes are priced lower than most performance shoes and competitively with other canvas shoe manufacturers.

- *Place*

  Vans are sold by a nationwide network of more than 6,100 independent shoe, sporting goods, and apparel stores and internationally in 35 countries.

- *Promotion*

  Print has been the primary medium for Vans, which has traditionally advertised in youth-oriented fashion magazines and dedicated sports magazines for skateboarding and Motocross. Vans are regularly featured on covers and in fashion layouts of magazines such as *SpinFashion, Mirabella, Seventeen*, and *Young & Modern*. Transit posters and outdoor boards are used in Europe and selected U.S. metropolitan areas. Television commercials have appeared on MTV and ESPN. A high percentage of promotion dollars have been dedicated to persuading retailers to carry the Vans line, in trade publications such as *Footwear News*. Direct mail targets particular lines to special market segments identified through subscription mailing lists and shopping center client lists.

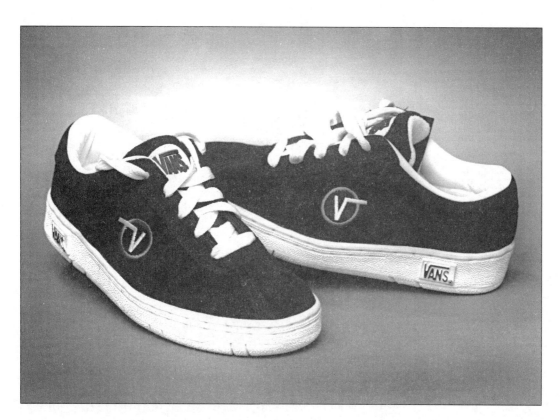

- *Problem:*

  The sneaker category contains so many competitors that consumers get confused with the plethora of choices available. In spite of low prices and availability, Vans' image as a skateboarder's shoe has limited its collegiate sales. However, the company considers its new line of shoes appropriate for campus wear and wants to target students attending two- and four-year colleges in ten collegiate regions (Northern Illinois, Boston, Atlanta, Southern California, Northern California, Florida, Michigan, Central Texas, Southern Arizona, and Central Colorado).

- *Objective:*

  Your agency has been retained to develop a campus-oriented advertising and promotional campaign directed at college students and local retailers. You decide to test-market the campaign on your campus for future roll-out to other markets nationwide.

ARM & HAMMER TOOTHPASTE

COMPANY BACKGROUND

Founded in 1846 by Church & Dwight, Arm & Hammer is a unique company that manufactures consumer and industrial products and is headquartered in Princeton, New Jersey. Using the Arm & Hammer trademark, the company liberated baking soda from the confines of its famous yellow box and expanded into such products as toothpaste, laundry detergent, cat litter, carpet deodorizer, air freshener, and antiperspirants. In 1994, over 1,000 employees worldwide generated annual revenues in excess of $500 million. Manufacturing boxes with recycled paper, Arm & Hammer recently developed the technology to purify drinking water and reduce smokestack pollution. In 1989, Arm & Hammer introduced the first baking-soda–enriched toothpaste, and in 1994 it added a peroxide-enriched toothpaste called Peroxicare.

MARKET

As a premium-priced product, Arm & Hammer Baking Soda Toothpaste is most popular with older consumers who attribute value to the brand. Ranking eleventh among brands with the highest perceived value, Arm & Hammer is a familiar brand to "Baby Boomers," who made an easy transition to its toothpaste in the early 1990s.

MARKETING MIX

- *Product*

  Producing a strong sensation of cleanness, a "fresh from the dentist feeling of clean," Arm & Hammer toothpaste contains more than 60% baking soda, compared with less than 30% for Colgate and Crest. Baking soda toothpaste comes in four varieties: paste-mint flavor, gel-mint flavor, tartar control paste-mint flavor, and tartar control gel-mint flavor. The product claims to fight gum disease, keep teeth and gums healthy, taste great, and be all natural. The product is packaged in standard and stand-up tubes.

- *Price*

  Suggested retail prices in the U.S. are between $2.29 and $2.79.

- *Place*

  Arm & Hammer distributes nationwide to supermarkets, pharmacies, and convenience stores, and worldwide, where prices and locations vary according to market conditions.

- *Promotion*

  The majority of Arm & Hammer's advertising buys are in network television, cable, network radio, magazines, and newspaper inserts. In 1993, baking soda toothpaste was launched in the U.K. with television and magazine advertising.

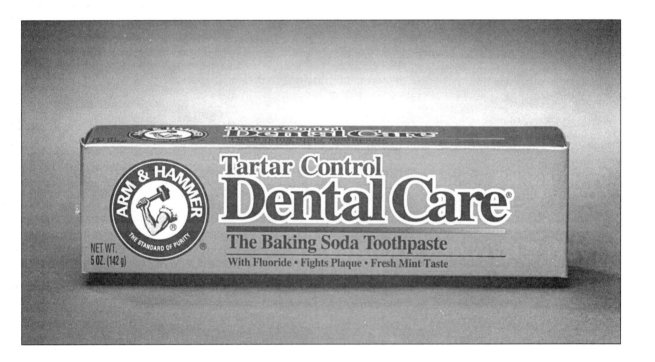

AGENCY ASSIGNMENT

- *Problem:*

  The toothpaste industry accounts for $1.43 billion in sales, with Arm & Hammer ranking fourth among bestsellers. Four years after its launching in 1989, Arm & Hammer's market share peaked at 9.9%, making it the leading U.S. baking soda toothpaste brand, with more than 20 million users. However, the product lost market share in 1994 and 1995, dropping off to 8.2%.

  Facing challenges by technological advances such as triclosan and discounted pricing available at warehouse outlet stores, Arm & Hammer is looking for ways to increase its popularity among consumers less familiar with its brand equity.

- *Objective:*

  Your agency has been asked to develop a campaign and retail promotion for collegiate consumers that will increase awareness of the Arm & Hammer brand name and educate male and female consumers about the environmental superiority of its toothpaste products. The client insists upon campus promotional tie-ins with organizations and other well-accepted products. Its markets are international, but your campus has been selected as a test-market for the projected national roll-out.

Part II:
Choosing an Agency Role

client

career interest

preferences
& talents

organizing
the agency

After reading about agency jobs in your text, review the positions presented in this section and select the one that resembles what you would like to do when you graduate, or one that capitalizes on a talent you already have. If you are undecided, select the research position, which offers an opportunity to influence all agency decisions.

ROLE DESCRIPTIONS

- *Account Executive (AE)*

  As an AE, you assume the greatest responsibility for the agency's performance. You assign tasks, make certain that deadlines are met, are responsible for putting together the final plans book, and are generally accountable for the agency's output. You evaluate agency members' performance and make final determinations in case of disputes or problems. *For this job you must have the time, energy, and commitment to be the agency's driving force.*

- *Account Manager*

  As an account manager, you assist the AE and assume that role if the AE is absent. You keep all written records and act as the recorder for attendance and activities of agency members. You are also responsible for keeping track of deadlines and making certain that tasks are completed properly. *Take this job if you are organized, efficient, and can work well with an AE.*

- *Researcher(s)*

  Researchers are responsible for collecting surveys, analyzing results, and preparing a research report for the advertising plan. Researchers also must spend time in the library updating the situation analysis and communicating that information to the agency members. *This important job is ideal for people who enjoy gathering data and tracking down facts.*

- *Media Planner(s)*

  Using the media suggested by the team, planners make specific selections of magazines, newspapers, billboard locations, radio stations, TV stations, direct mail pieces, and Internet home pages. You also prepare a media schedule and make budget allocations for media placement. *If you have a head for figures and like negotiations, this is the position for you.*

MANAGEMENT TEAM

RESEARCH TEAM

MEDIA TEAM

CREATIVE TEAM

- *Artist(s)*

  Develop concepts and create executions for advertisements. *If you have some artistic talent and computer graphic knowledge, take this job.*

- *Writer(s)*

  Compose headlines and print ad copy, and scripts and storyboards for electronic media. *English minors and people with a flair for prose should seriously consider this position.*

  Artists and writers work together to prepare print ads and broadcast commercials. With direction from the agency on strategy, the creative team develops advertising and promotion executions. Print and broadcast ads are used for the client pitch and are included in the plans book. You may be responsible for presenting the creative plan to the client.

PROMOTION AND PUBLICITY TEAM

- *Sales and Event Promotions Director*

  Because promotions are an important part of each campaign, promoters must be inventive and develop unique ways to reach the target market with product samples and positive image-building devices. *If you like directing consumer behaviors, this job is for you.*

- *Public Relations Director*

  To reach the target market through non-paid promotion, you supplement the campaign with news releases and media program placements for company representatives. *You should like behind-the-scenes activities and have some writing ability for this job.*

PRODUCTION TEAM

- *Coordinator(s)*

  Assemble the campaign plan and the creative executions. *If you are computer literate and have some experience in graphics, this is a good job for you.*

Preference Sheet: Selecting a Client and Agency Role

Complete this form and hand it in to the instructor, who will assign you to a group and position that adheres as closely as possible to your preferences.

Your name _____ Phone number _____

Which client would you prefer? _____
Why? _____
_____

Which role would you prefer? _____
Why? _____
_____

What is your second choice for an agency role? _____
Third choice? _____

What is your career interest? _____
_____

What is your major? _____

Do you have any special talents, needs, or interests we should know about? _____
_____
_____

target market

Part III:
Preliminary Planning Activities

research

conducting surveys

public relations

creating

strategies

PLANNING ACTIVITY 1   Organizing the Agency

A. As your group meets for the first time, discuss your roles and exchange personal communication information. Once you get acquainted, fill out this roster to keep as a record of your agency's members and their roles.

The name of our agency is _____

Member's name	Role/Team	Phone
	AE _____	
	Account manager _____	

B. Suggest a logo design for your agency and share it with the art director, who should make a final selection for the group by your next meeting.

PLANNING ACTIVITY 2   Profiling the Target Market

This Planning Activity will help you to understand how agencies identify personal and environmental factors that influence the buying behavior of consumers. Develop a profile for collegiate consumers using the information in your textbook as a guide.

A. Provide a psychographic profile, including personality traits (innovators, early adopters, etc.) and lifestyle criteria (VALS 2).

- Personality traits

- Lifestyle criteria

B. List at least three characteristics that can be used to segment the college market, and tell which of Maslow's needs would be appropriate to sell that segment a sports car.

Segment	Need
1. _____	_____
2. _____	_____
3. _____	_____

C. List three specific media preferred by this audience and reasons why.

Medium	Reason
1. _____	_____
2. _____	_____
3. _____	_____

Interest Inventory

Next to each of the following statements, place the letter of the response that best describes your feelings about that statement.

    a. Strongly agree
    b. Agree
    c. Neutral
    d. Disagree
    e. Strongly disagree

1. _____ My friends mean more to me than almost anything.
2. _____ I don't believe in "blowing my own horn" just to be heard.
3. _____ Searching for and finding what makes me feel happy is the most important thing in my life.
4. _____ I prefer to be by myself a lot of the time.
5. _____ A secure job and a good salary are number one for me.
6. _____ Chasing dreams is a waste of time and energy.
7. _____ I get furious when someone else tries to take credit for what I know I did.
8. _____ I really don't worry about a particular job or what I get for doing it as long as it's fair.

Scoring form:

Item	a	b	c	d	e	Score	Need Scale
5	5	4	3	2	1		
8	1	2	3	4	5	= ____	Safety/security
1	5	4	3	2	1		
4	1	2	3	4	5	= ____	Belonging/social
2	1	2	3	4	5		
7	5	4	3	2	1	= ____	Self-esteem
3	5	4	3	2	1		
6	1	2	3	4	5	= ____	Self-actualization

Scores range from 2 to 10 on each of the four need scales. The four need scores correspond to the higher level needs of Maslow's hierarchy. Does your highest score reflect what you consider to be your greatest need?_____

Some information about our products is accessible from publications, the Web, and other secondary sources. But for account planners to understand something about why consumers purchase a product, a first-hand visit to the retailer is valuable research. Visiting a shoe store or drug emporium to see all the available choices and how people choose among them is the point of this activity. The result will be a benefit segment chart of the products in your category by benefit and audience segment.

People buy products for different reasons. Take shampoo, for instance. Teens often buy it for cosmetic reasons so they "look better;" moms buy the "no tears" kind for their kids; some men get shampoo to fight dandruff; folks with large families choose a store brand for the low price; other buyers prefer an "all natural" product. A benefit segment chart for shampoo might look like this:

Benefit	Brand	Buyer
Price	Generic	Budget-conscious
Natural ingredients	Aveda, Ecco Bella	Health-conscious
Looks	Prell, Norell, Suave	Appearance-conscious
Medicinal	Head 'n Shoulders	Dandruff victims
Mild/baby	Johnson & Johnson	Parents
Designer image	Vidal Sassoon	Status- or image-conscious

A. Visit a local retailer carrying your product category, preferably one near campus where your audience shops. Spend about 30 minutes watching who buys what.

B. Check out the available inventory and develop a benefit segment chart below.

Benefit	Brand	Buyer

C. How does segmenting for benefits help you understand your consumer?

PLANNING ACTIVITY 4

Primary Research:
Conducting a Survey

In order to learn about consumer attitudes towards their client's product or service, many agencies conduct primary research using surveys to sample the population.

The parts of the survey and order of presentation are:

1. Introduction
   - Identify yourself
   - State the purpose
2. Directions
   - Tell how to answer each question
3. Questions
   - Likert scales
   - Adjective checklist
   - Ranking
4. Respondent demographics
   - Sex
   - Class level

A. Make six copies of the client survey for your product provided in this *Planner* (or construct one with your agency) and have five students fill them out. Use the extra copy to tally the responses from the completed surveys you collect. Give the tally, with your name, to the researcher in your agency.

The agency researcher will write up a report for the ad plan, including: purpose of the research, sample, results, and an overview of what the research contributed to your understanding of the perceptions of the target market about the product/service. This report should be given to the Account Manager for safe keeping.

B. Write a summary what you learned from the survey research activity.

Survey on Casual Footwear

My advertising class is researching student attitudes and preferences regarding casual footwear. Please take a few minutes to fill out the survey. Thank you.

1. When you think of canvas shoes (not pricey athletic shoes), what brand name comes to mind?
    _____

2. Rank in order of preference (1 being the most favorite) your brand preferences in casual shoes:

    _____ Keds
    _____ Vans
    _____ Converse
    _____ LA Gear
    _____ Other _____

3. Circle the adjectives that best describe your attitude about Vans sneakers.

    | customized | trendy | impractical | for skateboarders | comfortable |
    | for teens | who cares? | wonderful | affordable | impractical |

4. Place the numbers 1 and 2 in front of the two incentives that might tempt you to consider trying Vans shoes or buying another pair.
    _____ Free laces
    _____ Sixth pair free
    _____ Limited time student discount
    _____ Sweepstakes or contest

In the next four questions, indicate how important each of the items is to your purchase decision for casual shoes with the corresponding number.

very	somewhat	not very	not at all
4	3	2	1

_____ 5. How important is style ?   _____ 6. How important is comfort?
_____ 7. How important is price?   _____ 8. How important is image?

9. How likely are you to buy a pair of Vans in the next six months? (circle one)
    very likely   likely   unlikely   very unlikely

10. Tell us about yourself by checking the appropriate descriptors.
    _____ male   _____ female
    _____ freshman _____ sophomore _____ junior _____ senior _____ graduate

Survey on Toothpaste

My advertising class is researching student attitudes and preferences regarding toothpaste. Please take a few minutes to fill out the survey. Thank you.

1. When you think of toothpaste with baking soda, what brand name comes to mind?

    _____

2. Circle the adjectives that best describe your experience with Arm & Hammer products.

    for baking   for the refrigerator   mom/dad used them   never heard of any

    no experience   positive   extensive   limited

3. Tell how important each item is to your toothpaste purchase by writing in the correct number.

very important	somewhat important	not important
5	3	1

    _____ flavor

    _____ baking soda

    _____ peroxide

    _____ all natural ingredients

    _____ environmentally responsible company

    _____ price

4. Place the numbers 1 and 2 in front of the two incentives that might tempt you to try or re-buy Arm & Hammer baking soda or peroxide toothpaste.

    _____ Free toothbrush

    _____ Sixth tube free

    _____ T-shirt premium with proof of purchase

    _____ 50-cents-off coupon

5. How likely are you to purchase Arm & Hammer baking soda or peroxide toothpaste in the next three months? (circle one)

    very likely   likely   unlikely   very unlikely

6. Tell us about yourself: _____ male _____ female

    _____ freshman _____ sophomore _____ junior _____ senior _____ graduate

    THANK YOU FOR YOUR TIME

PLANNING ACTIVITY 5   Secondary Research: *Developing a Situation Analysis*

Because circumstances and events change so rapidly, agencies conduct secondary research to determine what social, economic, or other uncontrollable factors will affect strategic elements of the advertising plan. To obtain the most recent information on your client, use the library to research information needed for the situation analysis. Fill in the necessary information using a business periodical index on CD-ROM, NEXUS, and the Internet (see page 31 for relevant Internet addresses). Begin your research by looking up the product category or industry and then search the company name. Use *AdWeek* and *AdAge* to research past and current advertising campaigns of the client's competitors.

A. INDUSTRY OVERVIEW

The size of my client's industry (shoes or toothpaste) by sales volume is $ _____ .

Sales in $ millions over the past five years for that industry are:

1990 $_____   1992 $_____   1994 $_____

1991 $_____   1993 $_____   1995 $_____

Economic impacts on the industry are _____

_____

Social influences on the industry are _____

_____

The impact of technology on the industry is _____

_____

B. PRODUCT EVALUATION

The client's share of the market is _____ %.

Past advertising has appeared on/in (check *Leading National Advertisers* for media vehicles and expenditures) _____

_____ _____

The product is differentiated from its competitors by its _____

_____

Product features are _____

Product benefits are _____

The product's strengths are _____

The product's weakness is _____

Consumer attitudes toward the product as reported by the survey are

_____

_____

In addition to consulting secondary sources, you are advised to develop a first-hand familiarity with your client. Buy or try the product. As a result of your primary research with the product, what is your attitude toward it?

_____

_____

C. COMPETITIVE ANALYSIS

Competitors who compete directly are those making the same products. Indirect competitors vie for the same consumer dollar, but the product may be a different type or come in a different form.

The direct or major competitors for the client are:

_____

_____

Minor or indirect competition includes:

_____

_____

Direct competitors advertise on/in the following media:

_____

They feature these promotions:

_____

Top-of-mind awareness of survey respondents shows that the competition is:

_____

D. COLLABORATE

Share this information with your group to make certain that you all have similar facts and information.

On-Line Marketing and Advertising Web Site Addresses

AdLib
www.slip.net/ddynabus/adkub/htm
Reviews of current commercials.

AdRap
www.magicmedia/adrap.htm
Canadian executives' thoughts on advertising.

Advertising Age Online
www.adage.com
Daily news updates and employment opportunities.

American Association of Advertising Agencies
www.commercepark.com/aaaa
Updates on legislation.

BizInfo
www.dnai.com/sharrow/enter.htm
Sex in ads; ad parodies; Java tips.

Communication Arts
www.commarts.com
Production contacts; job listings; examples of good print ads.

Direct Marketing Association
www.the-dma.org/dmef
List of programs and services.

IDEABANK
204.214.139.14/ideabanc.htm
Radio's largest promotional database.

International Advertising Association
www.usa.com/homepage.htm
Reviews the state of the industry; *Communications World* online.

IPREX
www.iprex.com
Directory of PR firms by area of expertise.

KGB Media
www.kgbmedia.com
Features on media and pop culture; celebrity interviews; cool graphics.

As a preliminary exercise to brainstorming with your group, take some time to think about a "Big Idea" for your client's product by completing this Planning Activity, which demonstrates how to develop three different creative strategies: *positioning, USP,* and *imaging.*

A. POSITIONING

Think about the product in terms of the problem it will solve for college students. For instance, the problem Diet Coke solves is how to quench your thirst without adding calories to your diet. It solves that problem by using sugar substitutes instead of sugar as a sweetener in the beverage.

The problem the product or service solves for the user is how to _____

_____

The product or service solves that problem by _____

_____

A *positioning strategy* for advertising the product or service is to position the product as the best solution to that problem. A Diet Coke commercial might show a user of another product reacting unfavorably to the taste with a broad facial grimace. Diet Coke positions itself as the "best-tasting" diet cola with face distortions as a "Big Idea."

Write a "Big Idea" for your client that is based on a positioning strategy.

Think about the product/service's benefit for your target audience. The main benefit for college

students is _____

B. UNIQUE SELLING PROPOSITION

A strategy for advertising the product/service using the benefit is to dramatize the product's physical *feature* that produces that benefit—its unique selling position (USP). For instance, truck users want a flatbed that has lots of room for hauling. The *USP strategy* dramatizes how much bigger your truck is than the competition's truck. A "Big Idea" is loading both trucks with puppies, showing how many more pups will fit in your truck than in the competition's truck.

Now write your own "Big Idea" for your client using the USP strategy.

C. BRAND OR USER IMAGE

Think about the product's *benefit* again, this time a benefit that is *not* physical. Maybe the benefit is excitement or social status. An *imaging strategy* borrows excitement or social status from something else and transfers it to the brand, such as using a roller-coaster ride to dramatize the excitement of a new lipstick; or using the social status of a large mansion to imply that your brand of watch is evidence of the wearer's success; or borrowing the lifestyle of a exuberant skiers as proof that your brand of ski wear is preferable to your consumer segment.

Write a "Big Idea" for your client using a brand image strategy for print. Include a description of what quality you will borrow to transfer to your product.

Write a "Big Idea" for your client using a user image strategy for television.

One of the most interesting and imaginative aspects of putting together a campaign is creating the ads. But while we love to let our talents go wild, clients demand executions that will achieve the advertising communication objectives. This Planning Activity is designed to see how close you can come to being creative within the limitations imposed by the objective. In other words, if your objective is to persuade the audience that your product is very different from the others and your strategy is positioning, your executions must persuade with a physical feature.

Objective:

Strategy:

Tactic: 1.   Half-page black and white newspaper ad
           2.   Full-page full color magazine ad

A.   First, develop a thumbnail sketch for two *print* ads for your client that will achieve your objectives and strategy. Make certain that you consider all the design elements made in your text.

B.   Next, write a headline and a few lines of copy for each ad. Make certain your copy follows the text guidelines, and that your ads reflect the objectives you established earlier.

C.   If you are handy with a computer, make a finished ad. If not, just sketch out your ideas. Sketch your ideas here, or attach your completed thumbnails or executions to this sheet.

A. TELEVISION:
Commercials are more complicated to develop than print ads because they require action and dialogue to communicate the advertising message. Concepts for commercials begin with a storyboard and script. If you want to try your hand at a thumbnail storyboard, great. If not, just jot down your ideas for a commercial for your client, again staying on strategy to achieve your objectives.

Objective:

Strategy:

Tactic: :30 spot for cable

(see next page)

B. RADIO

Next, try your hand at a radio spot. Include the audio directions and script format suggested in your text.

Objective:

Strategy:

Tactic: :30 spot for a rock music station

PLANNING ACTIVITY 9 — Media Planning and Scheduling

A. Explain how appropriate each medium is for your target audience and why.

Medium	Very	Not very	Reason
Network TV			
Cable TV			
Local radio			
Magazines			
College newspaper			
Direct mail			
Outdoor			
Transit			
Point-of-purchase			
Internet			

B. For your client, what are the advantages and disadvantages of each type of scheduling?
   Flighting ————————————————————————————————————
   Pulsing ——————————————————————————————————————
   Continuous ————————————————————————————————————

C. Collaborate
   With your group, decide upon media objectives and choice of media vehicles for your client.

PLANNING ACTIVITY 10   Sales Promotions and Tie-Ins

A few years ago, the largest budget allocations for advertisers were for buying media. Today, advertisers allocate the majority of their budgets to promotions because effectiveness is more easily measured. As a result, agencies have developed strategies to tie media ads directly to promotional activities. Sales promotions act as incentives for consumers to buy and serve as reinforcements for media advertising.

A. If your product is new to your consumers, *trial* promotions are used. Suggest three trial tactics suitable for your client's audience.

    1. _____

    2. _____

    3. _____

B. When you want to reward loyal users, *usage* promotions are used. Suggest three usage tactics suitable for your client's audience.

    1. _____

    2. _____

    3. _____

C. Similar to joining with a retailer for cooperative advertising, promotional tie-ins connect a product with an event, or place their product in a film for exposure—beers embrace sporting events, and Pepsi was very prominent in *Top Gun*. An appropriate event or film placement for my client

is _____

because _____

D. Promotional products, free gifts to loyal customers or frequent users, also enhance brand equity— Starbucks gives coffee mugs to its distributors, and *Sunset Magazine* rewards regular subscribers with beach towels. An appropriate promotional item for your client to give its _____ is a

_____ because _____

A. Mailing lists are crucial for developing direct mail solicitations. Suggest two sources you might use to obtain mailing lists to reach your client's audience.

1. _____

2. _____

B. Direct mail pieces are often discarded before the intended audience reads them because they are not well designed. Describe how you would design a direct mail piece offering your client's product to one segment of your target audience so it won't end up in the trash.

C. Your client decides to put a home page on the Internet to answer questions and receive feedback from consumers. For consumers to take the time to connect with a manufacturer, they need some stimulation. Manufacturers may provide locations of local retailers carrying the product, or solicit participation in a user group discussion. What type of advertising message would you suggest for your client to stimulate on-line feedback from collegiate audiences?

PLANNING ACTIVITY 12   Public Relations

Building brand recognition and equity requires more than product advertising and sales promotion. To reach all the publics of a company, public relations activities must produce a variety of collateral materials.

A. Using your text as a guide, suggest an appropriate collateral piece for each of your client's publics listed below.

Public	Collateral piece
Shareholders	_____
Employees	_____
Media	_____
Potential employees	_____

Corporations often want to enhance their community image, to "give back" to the city or state of their headquarters location, or other locations that employ large numbers of their employees. For each of the activities listed below, suggest an appropriate vehicle to create a favorable image for your client. Make certain that your suggestions correspond to the interests of the company (like sports or health), not simply interests in general.

Local sponsorship activity   _____
                                    (e.g., Little League team)

National sponsorship activity   _____
                                    (e.g., National Ballet performance)

An activity to promote health   _____
                                    (e.g., free testing for high cholesterol)

An activity to advocate   _____
environmental responsibility   (e.g., recycling)

An activity to advocate an idea   _____
or philosophy   (e.g., child abuse prevention)

B. Assume that your client is preparing to make an announcement about a new "breakthrough" product and has asked you to recommend an appropriate celebrity spokesperson to appear at the news conference. Who would you suggest and why?

Celebrity _____

Rationale _____

media strategy

Part IV:
Agency Meeting Agendas

creative

management team responsibilities

meetings

brain-storming

AGENCY ROSTER

Roster for the _____ **Agency**

AE _____   Account Manager _____

Research Team Members   (name & phone)

_____ (leader)

_____

_____

Media Team Members

_____ (leader)

_____

_____

Creative Team Members

_____ (leader)

_____

_____

_____

_____

Promotion and Publicity Team Members

_____ (leader)

_____

_____

_____

Production Team Members

_____ (leader)

_____

_____

MANAGEMENT TEAM RESPONSIBILITIES

Account Executive is _____

Your responsibilities are to:

- Preside over agency meetings and lead the discussion or exercise as assigned.

- Attend at least one meeting of each team, and keep in touch with team leaders to check on team progress.

- Obtain materials for plans book from all team leaders as they complete their tasks and draft the information into sections. Use the example in the appendix of this *Planner* as a guide.

- Stay alert to problems or disagreements, and see your instructor if you need advice. You can fire a member if her/his team members file a petition for termination with reasons. Usually this process serves to work out the problem, and the person ends up not being fired. Advise your group of their option to fire a team member.

- Write the final plans book and make certain that the production team has one made for each member and one for the instructor by the date of your presentation.

Agency Manager is _____

Your responsibilities are to:

- Cover for the AE when she is not available for a meeting.

- Keep a record of who comes to the general meetings.

- Collect worksheets and record who handed them in; return worksheets to agency members.

- Read the agenda prior to each meeting to make certain all the business is taken care of before you adjourn.

- When appropriate, hand in your information to the instructor after each agency meeting.

MEETING AND ASSIGNMENT ROSTER

Responsible for checking attendance and assignments is _____

For each person in your agency, circle the general agency meetings each attends and the assignments each turns in.

Name	Meetings	Planning Activities
_____	1 2 3 4 5 6 7 8	2 3 4 5 6 7 8 9 10 11 12
_____	1 2 3 4 5 6 7 8	2 3 4 5 6 7 8 9 10 11 12
_____	1 2 3 4 5 6 7 8	2 3 4 5 6 7 8 9 10 11 12
_____	1 2 3 4 5 6 7 8	2 3 4 5 6 7 8 9 10 11 12
_____	1 2 3 4 5 6 7 8	2 3 4 5 6 7 8 9 10 11 12
_____	1 2 3 4 5 6 7 8	2 3 4 5 6 7 8 9 10 11 12
_____	1 2 3 4 5 6 7 8	2 3 4 5 6 7 8 9 10 11 12
_____	1 2 3 4 5 6 7 8	2 3 4 5 6 7 8 9 10 11 12
_____	1 2 3 4 5 6 7 8	2 3 4 5 6 7 8 9 10 11 12
_____	1 2 3 4 5 6 7 8	2 3 4 5 6 7 8 9 10 11 12
_____	1 2 3 4 5 6 7 8	2 3 4 5 6 7 8 9 10 11 12
_____	1 2 3 4 5 6 7 8	2 3 4 5 6 7 8 9 10 11 12
_____	1 2 3 4 5 6 7 8	2 3 4 5 6 7 8 9 10 11 12
_____	1 2 3 4 5 6 7 8	2 3 4 5 6 7 8 9 10 11 12
_____	1 2 3 4 5 6 7 8	2 3 4 5 6 7 8 9 10 11 12
_____	1 2 3 4 5 6 7 8	2 3 4 5 6 7 8 9 10 11 12
_____	1 2 3 4 5 6 7 8	2 3 4 5 6 7 8 9 10 11 12
_____	1 2 3 4 5 6 7 8	2 3 4 5 6 7 8 9 10 11 12

AGENCY AGENDA — First Meeting: *Organizing Your Agency and Meeting Team Members*

The Account Executive leads the general meetings.

1. **Introductions.**
   Since this is your first meeting as an agency, it's a good idea to let members introduce themselves, beginning with the AE. Each member should record the names and phone numbers of other members on the roster provided in Planning Activity 1.

2. **Teams.**
   The agency will be divided into six teams that will meet periodically to address specific tasks. Each team will elect a leader to be the liaison with the AE and direct team activity. Team meetings follow agency meetings when they are scheduled on the agenda. Teams may also meet outside of class to complete specific activities.

3. **Agency name.**
   Creating a name for the agency will unify your group under a single identity. Members should suggest names, then select the one preferred by the majority of the group. Members who want to design a logo for the agency should prepare their concept by the next meeting to share with the group. When you have a name and logo, the AE will hand it in to the instructor.

4. **About Planning Activities (PAs).**
   The account manager is responsible for collecting and recording completed PAs. Planning Activities are to be completed by each member and shared with the group or team during meetings. Exercises are collected on the due date; no late papers are accepted by managers. If students have an illness, have them speak directly to the instructor.

5. **The planning process.**
   The campaign planning process—activities and meetings—corresponds directly to the material discussed in your book and presented in class. If at first you are confused about your role in that process, you're not alone. However, most students confirm that after a few meetings your apprehension will dissolve and excitement will grow as you approach the competitive "client pitch" finale.

1. **Record PAs 2, 3, & 4.**
   Audience profiles, benefit segments and survey tally sheets (PAs 2, 3, & 4) will be collected from each member (not the surveys, just the tallies) and recorded on the roster at the beginning of this Part. After checking, survey tallies are forwarded to the research team leader.

2. **Discussion.**
   During this meeting, members share what they learned about the audience and the product from the audience profile, benefit segmentation, and survey activities. Use the following questions to direct the discussion; jot down your group's consensus after each one.

   a. What media are suitable to the lifestyle of your target audience? Why?

   b. What biases will advertising to this target market need to overcome?

   c. Which adjectives might be used to promote the product?

   d. What clues did the research provide for differentiating your product from its competitors?

3. **Research team meeting.**
   Following the agency meeting, members of the research team will meet to analyze all the survey tallies and develop a research report for the plans book. Survey result totals should be shared with the agency at your next meeting. Use the agenda for the research team meeting located in the Team Agenda section (Part V).

1. Record PA 5.

2. **Discuss secondary research results.**

   a. What did you learn about your client's industry?

   b. What did you learn about the product?

   c. What did you learn about the competition?

   d. How will you use this information?

3. **Research team report.**
   The research team leader will explain the results of the survey.

4. **Discuss primary research results.**

   a. What problems surfaced in the research?

   • Audience perception or attitude problems

   • Product awareness problems

   • Other problems

   b. What are the implications of the research for the creative strategy?

   • For positioning the product

   • For portraying the audience or lifestyle

   • For characterizing the product benefit

1. **Record PAs 6, 7, & 8.**
   A member of the creative team will use PAs 7 & 8 for its team meeting, which follows.

2. **Brainstorm.**
   This activity is an excellent way to stimulate creative thinking. Using PA 6 as a starting point, members of the agency should throw out suggestions for a "Big Idea" at random. Don't discuss or disregard any of the ideas; just let them flow. The AE will record your ideas. After 15 minutes or so, go back over the ideas and have people discuss the merit of each one. Put stars next to the ideas that the group liked best.

   Notes on the "Big Idea"

3. **Creative team meeting.**
   Following the agency meeting, members of the creative team will meet to further discuss the "Big Idea" and its execution by building upon the brainstorming activity. Make certain you collect the agency members' Planning Activities. Use the agenda for the creative team meeting located in the Team Agenda section.

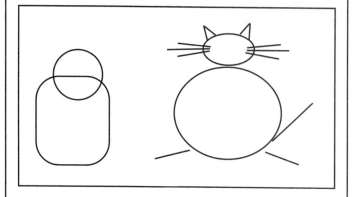

FOR THE CAT THAT WON'T FIT IN THE HAT

sadjshdfdhjdhdgijkhgkghfdkgdjk   sadjshdfdhjdhdgijkhgkghfdkgdjk

dfsjfsffsddsjkdlsfjgdkdshjssskehdje   dfsjfsffsddsjkdlsfjgdkdshjssskehdje

sadjshdfdhjdhdgijkhgkghfdkgdjk   sadjshdfdhjdhdgijkhgkghfdkgdjk

SLENDER CAT

Courtesy of Shirley Catalina.

A *thumbnail* is used during the conceptual stage of producing an ad. Using the computer as a sketch pad, a student outlined his concept of a print ad for Slender Cat, a dietary food for overweight felines.

Pagemaker was used to produce this ad for a student urging citizens to conserve water during a recent drought in Northern California.

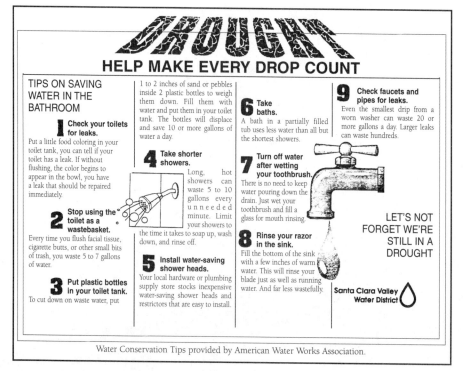

Courtesy of Santa Clara Valley Water District.

Testimonial ads were chosen by these students to express their feelings about a product. Do the advertisements reflect the stated objectives and strategies?

Client: B.U.M.
Objective: Create a brand image
Strategy: Contrast the word "bum" with the brand name

Client: D'Addario guitar strings
Objective: Change the attitude about the product from "high brow" to casual
Strategy: Show how the product fits into the college lifestyle

What's Wrong With Being a B.U.M.?

Get up. Go to school. Get a job. Get a life. Don't have fun. Work. Work. Work. What do you want to do, end up a bum?

Well, I get up. I go to school. I have a job. And a life. But I still manage to have fun, and being a bum has a lot to do with it.

B.U.M. Equipment makes sportswear for all types of casual activities. I can be a basketball bum. Or a baseball bum. I can be a hang gliding bum or a rollerblading bum. If those sound like too much work, I can lie in the sun and be a beach bum. It's up to me. People will never stop telling me what to do, but at least they can't tell me what to do it in.

Being a bum is comfortable. It's fashionable.
And best of all, it's fun.

For a free catalog of bum equipment, mail this coupon

Name _____ Sex _____ Age _____

Address _____

Telephone _____

b.u.m. equipment

Courtesy of Stuart Moore.

Good Music Makes Good Times

 I don't play my guitar too often. It's more of a hobby. But I take my playing seriously.

So when I get the chance to strum a few chords, I don't want a dull sound. I just want to relax and play some good music.

With D'Addario strings I know I can rely on that bright, crisp tone every time I pick up my guitar.

And when I sound good, I feel good.

D'Addario®
Escape from the day and play.

Courtesy of J. D'Addario Company Inc. and Raymond Winkler.

1. Record PA 9.

2. **Creative team report.**
   Creative team leader tells the group which creative ideas they have selected and their choices for executions based on preliminary media identification.

3. **Identify media classes.**
   Discuss which media classes are appropriate for the client to target a college audience. Make certain that you look at both the positive and negative aspects of the medium, such as cost, availability, ability to reach students, and likelihood that students will use it. Come up with at least three that you will use for your campaign.

   Based on your analysis in PA 7, select the three most appropriate media for targeting college students and explain why.

Medium	*Rationale*
•	
•	
•	

4. **Specify media vehicles.**
   For each medium you selected, suggest a specific vehicle, such as radio format, TV shows, specific magazines, Web site, outdoor location, etc. Record your decisions:

   -
   -
   -

5. **Media team meeting.**
   Following the agency meeting, members of the media team will meet to finalize media decisions. Use the agenda for the media team meeting located in the Team Agenda section.

AGENCY AGENDA

Sixth Meeting: *Identifying Promotions and PR Functions*

1. Record PAs 10, 11, & 12.

2. **Media team report.**
   Inform the agency about your media decisions.

3. **Determine sales promotions.**
   Exchange ideas for trial and usage promotions.

4. **Discuss event promotion.**
   Suggest several event options and their benefits to achieving your advertising goals.

5. **Discuss direct mailings.**
   Discuss the kind of mailer that will appeal to students and how it should be designed (colors, typeface, visuals, etc.).

6. **Discuss promotional products.**

   a. What promotional products are appropriate for retailers?

   b. What promotional products would you suggest for your audience?

7. **Discuss public relations.**

   a. What type of collateral piece is most appropriate?

   b. What sponsorships will you consider?

   c. Who is an ideal spokesperson for the company?

8. **Promotion/PR team meeting.**
   Following the agency meeting, members of the promotion/PR team will meet to finalize promotion and PR decisions. Use the agenda located in the Team Agenda section.

AGENCY AGENDA — Final Meeting: *Public Relations and Presenter Elections*

1. **Promotion team report.**
   Promotion team leader discloses ideas selected and how they will be presented.

2. **Elect presenters.**
   Presenters are people who are confident and have some experience with public speaking or sales. They understand the product and can articulate the creative solutions to the advertising problems of the client. Presenters work hard and take responsibility for the outcome of all the group's work.

   Nominate four people and vote by having each member write down two choices. The account manager tabulates the votes.

   - The presenters are:

   - The alternate is:

3. **Discuss the presentation and plans book production.**

   a. The agency will make decisions about what the presenters should wear, and what visuals and technical equipment are needed for the presentation. Presenters work with production people to implement the group decision.

   b. Written reports from all teams will be assembled for the plans book; discuss the production team's role in this process. Use the Appendix as a guide for preparing your agency's book.

4. **Production team meeting.**
   Following the agency meeting, members of the production team will meet to determine how best they can assist the management team with the plans book and the presenters with creative executions and visual aids.

research

creative

workplan

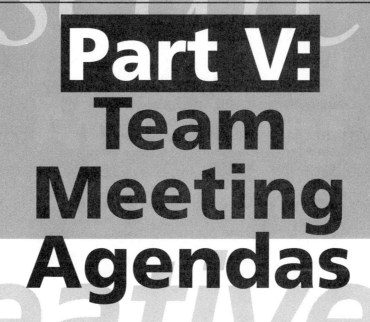

**Part V:
Team
Meeting
Agendas**

promotion/
PR

media

production

1. **Select a leader.**
    The leader directs the team activities, assigns tasks, calls meetings, and keeps track of progress. The leader for your team is _____ .

2. **Analyze the survey results.**
    Your team deals with the primary research results gathered through the survey. The agency manager will provide you with survey tallies; from there you must analyze the survey data. Use the following steps as a guide.

    For both Vans and Arm & Hammer surveys:
    a. *Tabulate top-of-mind brand awareness.* For question 1, total the mentions of each brand, and write down the top three. These are your competitors.
        1. _____
        2. _____
        3. _____

    b. *Calculate the percentage of the mentions for all brands named.* Design a pie chart to show the results.

    c. *Calculate the top three adjectives that were selected.* They are:
        1. _____
        2. _____
        3. _____

    d. *Identify the top two incentives.* They are:
        1. _____
        2. _____

    e. *Calculate the likelihood of buying:*
        * very likely + likely = _____
        * unlikely + very unlikely = _____

    f. *Calculate the totals for each demographic:*
        * females _____ males _____
        * _____ freshmen _____ sophomores _____ juniors _____ seniors _____ graduates

For the Vans survey only:

a. *Calculate brand preferences.* Count how many times each received a number 1.

- Favorite is _____
- Vans ranked _____ in the list of favorites

b. *Calculate the importance of benefits.* For questions 5–8, add the numbers for each benefit in each item. Record the totals below:

- _____ style
- _____ comfort
- _____ price
- _____ image

c. *Make a graph of the results.*

For the Arm & Hammer survey only:

a. *Calculate the importance of each feature in question 3.* Total the points for each item:

- ____ flavor
- ____ baking soda
- ____ peroxide
- ____ all natural ingredients
- ____ environmentally responsible company
- ____ price

b. *Make a graph of the results.*

3. **Agency communication.**
This research yields information that is needed by creative and promotion teams. Be prepared to discuss your findings at your next agency meeting.

4. **Write a report.**
The details of this survey need to be written up in a report for the advertising plan.
Follow these directions.

a. *Explain the sample.* Tell the who, what, where, and when of the collection and people who completed surveys. Use the demographic information from the surveys, and provide a pie chart to show the class ranking distribution; do not chart gender.

b. *Discuss the top-of-mind awareness of your client's brand.* Identify the competitors, and include the pie chart below the narrative.

c. *Discuss adjective references.* Talk about the implications of the adjectives for advertising the product/service.

d. *Reveal the importance of feature or benefit items.* Discuss what they suggest for advertising the product.

e. *Type the report and include professional visuals.* Label your report section "Primary Research" and give it to the AE of your agency. Your report will be used as a major part of the advertising plan.

TEAM AGENDA   Creative

1. **Select a leader.**
   The leader directs the team activities, assigns tasks, calls meetings, and keeps track of progress. The leader for your team is _____ .

2. **Develop a creative strategy.**
   Your team has the most important job in the agency because your advertising executions are what will convince the client to select your agency. Using PA 6 from your group members as well as your own ideas, decide upon a strategy and "Big Idea" for your client.

3. **Design specific executions.**
   Your team will need to meet several times to accomplish final drafts of your ads. Design several alternatives for your ads or spots so the presenters have options of what to produce for the presentation. Put print ads on slides or overhead transparencies; put radio spots on a cassette with music; present TV spots on video or as a storyboard on slides or transparencies. Promotional materials or direct mail pieces can also be reproduced on slides. Work with the production team to get them ready for the presentation.

4. **Prepare your portion of the plans book.**
   Make 8″ × 11″ copies of the creative executions for the plans book. Also, have one person write up a rationale for your ideas. The best way to do this is with a creative work plan (CWP). One example of a CWP is attached to use as a guide. Hand in your plan materials to the AE in time for her/him to prepare the entire plan that is handed in before the presentation.

5. **Agency communication.**
   Your ideas are important because the promotion and PR team must build its materials around your "Big Idea" and graphic elements. Be prepared to share your ideas at the next agency meeting.

Creative Work Plan (CWP) for Crystal Cola

Problem:
Client's perception; why
they need advertising.

Sales have declined since the
popularity of bottled water has
increased dramatically.

Consumer Problem:
A fact stated from the consumer's
point of view; what keeps the
consumer from buying or trying
the product.

People prefer healthy drinks
to caffeinated, caloric beverages.

Advertising Goal:
What you will do to overcome
the product and consumer problems?

Introduce "clear cola" as a water
and cola alternative.

Competition:
Who are they? What is their main
consumer benefit?

Iced tea, flavored waters.
Variety, taste, natural.

Target Market:
Who are the prime prospects?

Active adults 28–55.

"Big Idea":
Creative strategy; the promise to the
consumer of the benefits of your
product; what sets it apart from the
competition; your promise to the
consumer.

Light refreshment without
caffeine or harmful additives
that quenches thirst and
tastes great.

Radio Script Format

Client: _____ Product: _____

Writer: _____ Length: _____ seconds

Directions (Single sp. in clc)	SCRIPT (DBL sp. in CPS)
DIRECTIONS— AUDIO DIRECTIONS: **ACR or BOY #1 or JANE**. Identify who the speaker is each time the speaker changes. If it's the same character, don't repeat the identification each time the dialogue is broken, e.g., by SFX, music, etc. The first time the character or group is introduced, describe him or her (or them). **NAT SOUND** means "natural background" sounds viz. the setting in which the dialogue, etc., is occurring. Indicate what type of NAT SOUND is desired. **MUSIC DIRECTIONS:** Indicate a specific song & artist, or the type of music to be used. **SFX DIRECTIONS:** Indicate what SFX is to be used.	**SCRIPT COPY—**AUDIO DIRECTIONS: Direct the actor [using brackets in the copy] how fast the delivery should be, what tone of voice should be used., etc. NAT SOUND: Indicate [using brackets] where the NAT SOUND is to start, how long it's to run, when it's to fade, etc. MUSIC DIRECTIONS: Indicate [using brackets] where the music is to start, how long it's to run, when it's to stop or fade. SFX DIRECTIONS: Indicate [using brackets] where the SFX is to start, how long it's to run, when it's to stop, fade, etc.

The OUTSIDE MARGIN s 1 1/2".

EACH FRAME is
3" wide and 2 3/8" deep
using a 2 pt. line.
Either reproduce
or
cut from the
COMP FRAMES sheet.

EACH FRAME is
a color scene.
Draw in using black ink.
Then color.

#1 VIDEO DIRECTIONS: ES, CU,
COVER SHOT [of blueprint] [2 sec.]

AUDIO/DIALOGUE: Female ACR:
THE DREAM STARTS HERE
[MUSIC: classical, soft w/violins.
Estb. 3 secs., fade under]

#2 VIDEO DIRECTIONS: MATCH
DIS TO LS, COVER SHOT [1 sec.]

AUDIO/DIALOGUE: MALE ACR:
THE TECHNIQUE . . .

The DIRECTIONS &
AUDIO/DIALOGUE space is
3" wide x 2 5/8" deep.
Use 12 pt. type AUTO leading.
Set 1 1/2 picas below the bottom
edge of each frame.
SEE EXAMPLES TO THE LEFT

The MARGIN between the frames is 1".

The MARGIN between the frames is 1".

The OUTSIDE MARGIN s 1 1/2".

1. **Choose a leader.**
   The leader directs the team activities, assigns tasks, calls meetings, and keeps track of progress. The leader for your team is _____ .

2. **Develop a media plan.**
   Your team has the important task of developing a media plan. Using PA 9 from your group and research into the demographic appeal of specific media outlets you're considering (such as the information in the table below), develop a media buy for your client.

3. **Prepare a media schedule.**
   After you have decided upon the vehicles and the specific programs and time, put your choices into a media schedule.

4. **Determine budget allocations.**
   Using a pie chart, show what proportion you will spend on each medium. Remember that your budget is affected by the cost of buying the media, so be certain to calculate approximate costs using the information in your text or the SRDS as a guide. You should justify your media expenditures with appropriate rationale.

5. **Write a report.**
   Your section of the advertising plan is important. One person should be selected to write a rationale for the media you chose and for the expenditures you will make. Give this narrative, your pie chart, and the media schedule to the AE in time for her/him to prepare the plan.

6. **Agency communication.**
   Media buying has implications for promotions as well as creative. Be prepared to share your information with the agency at the next meeting.

With more competition, each broadcast TV network is trying to sharpen its appeal to the demographic groups that make up its core viewership. Here are recent prime-time rating breakdowns.

	ABC	CBS	FOX	NBC	UPN	WB
People 50 years old and older	7.1	9.7	2.7	8.0	1.3	Not available
Women 18–49 years old	6.1	5.1	4.8	7.9	1.7	1.4
Men 18–49 years old	5.0	3.2	4.2	5.6	1.8	1.0
Youths 12–17 years old	4.6	2.2	4.6	4.2	1.9	2.6

During the 1995–96 television season, one rating point equaled 959,000 households.
Sources: Nielsen Media Research, ABC, NBC, UPN, WB.

1. **Select a leader.**
   The leader directs the team activities, assigns tasks, calls meetings, and keeps track of progress. The leader for your team is _____ .

2. **Develop sales promotions.**
   Using PAs 10 and 11 prepared by members of your agency, select sales promotions and direct mail ideas that you think have merit. Develop the best ideas for the ad plan and the presentation. Come up with innovative ways to get your target audience to buy or try your product/service in both promotions and mail communications.

   - Obtain the artwork/logo/design materials from the creative team, and have the production team help you to produce a mail piece for the presentation. You can have it reproduced as an overhead transparency for the presentation, and the actual mail piece can be put into the plans book.

3. **Write the promotions report for the plans book.**
   Someone from your team will write up your ideas and a rationale for the plans book. Give the completed section to the AE in time for her/him to put it in the plan.

4. **Write a news release.**
   Someone must write a news release on your product. The audience is your school newspaper. Using the attached format and your textbook, prepare a release that tells about a promotional event or campus activity sponsored by your client. Give this release to your AE for the plan.

5. **Agency communication.**
   Share your decisions with the group at your last meeting, and help the presenters with information so they can discuss your promotions during the presentation.

News Release Format

When preparing your news release, follow these directions:

1. Use 1″ margins on all sides.

2. Place the address of the sender in the upper left-hand corner of the first page. Make certain your name and phone number are included.

3. Place FOR IMMEDIATE RELEASE on the right-hand side.

4. Begin the release 1/3 of the way down the page. The headline should be in all caps, underlined. Begin with the dateline (city where the release was written and the date separated by a colon, e.g., Boston: June 21, 1997).

5. Double-space the body of the release; indent paragraphs. Do not split paragraphs from one page to the next. Place the word "more" within dashes at the bottom of the page. Use the symbols #### at the end.

Company or Client Name
and Address go here
Contact: Your name
Phone:

FOR IMMEDIATE RELEASE

<u>HEADLINE GOES HERE IN ALL CAPS, UNDERLINED</u>

The city of origin dateline goes here—The body of the release begins one-third of the way down the page. Double-space for readability and editing.

Use normal indents and consistent spacing between paragraphs. Present all information in descending order of importance, ending with the least important items.

Remember to leave at least one-inch margins all around. Place a—more—at the end of the page when you go beyond one page. Do not break paragraphs or sentences in the middle.

####

TEAM AGENDA   Production

1. **Select a leader.**
   The leader directs the team activities, assigns tasks, calls meetings, and keeps track of progress. The leader for your team is _____ .

2. **Assign responsibilities.**
   Your team has a very important role for the agency presentation because all the materials the agency members have to present will be a direct result of your production skills. In addition, your ability to produce an attractive plans book will affect everyone's grade.

   - PowerPoint can be used to make slides or transparencies. The more professional your visual aids, the better chance the agency has of securing the client.

   - Check with media, creative, and promotion teams to see what materials they need for the presentation, and with the AE on what she/he needs for the plans book. Each person in the team should take a specific task and carry it through.

   - Communication with other teams in essential.

   - Give yourself enough time to get the job done.

Evaluation Sheet for _____ Agency

Evaluated by _____

This form will help the instructor judge each member's role in the overall team project. If you determine their involvement to be outstanding, award them a + mark; if it was satisfactory, an = mark should be awarded; assign a — mark if their contribution was minimal.

For each of the members in your agency, include the following information:

Member's name	Meetings attended	Activities recorded	Mark

Hand in this form as directed by your instructor.

| Evaluation Sheet for _____ | | | | **Team** |

Evaluated by _____

Your honest evaluation will help the instructor determine the role of each member of your team in the overall agency performance. For each member of your team, please rank each item:

+   indicates an outstanding effort
=   indicates a satisfactory effort
—   indicates a minimal contribution

Member's name	Effort	Attendance	Contribution	Overall

Hand in this form as directed by your instructor.

print ads

Part VI:
Practicing Your Skills

buying

event planning

media

targeting
an audience

broadcast

EXERCISE A   Advertising Classifications

Find an example of an advertisement for each of the following classifications as explained in your text. Mount the ads on a plain sheet of paper and include them in your notebook. Be prepared to discuss them in class.

1. **Target audiences**

    a. Consumer advertising:

    _____   _____   _____
    Publication name   *Date*   *Product/service*

    b. Business advertising:

    _____   _____   _____
    Publication name   *Date*   *Product/service*

2. **Purpose**

    a. Nonproduct, corporate, or institutional advertising:

    _____   _____   _____
    Publication name   *Date*   *Product/service*

    b. Noncommercial advertising:

    _____   _____   _____
    Publication name   *Date*   *Product/service*

    c. Action advertising:

    _____   _____   _____
    Publication name   *Date*   *Product/service*

    d. Awareness advertising:

    _____   _____   _____
    Publication name   *Date*   *Product/service*

1. **Options**
   For this exercise, you may choose either of the following options.
   a. Locate a medium-sized to large agency in your area in preparation for the following assignment.
   b. Research a national agency by consulting sources such as *Advertising Age* (www.adage.com), *Ad Week*, the "Red Book" of agencies (usually located at the reference desk in your university library), NEXUS, the business periodicals index on CD-ROM in the library, or by contacting the American Association of Advertising Agencies. (www.comercepark.com.aaaa).

2. **Assignment**
   Locate and record the following information:

   Agency name, phone, location: _____

   _____

   _____

   Name of the agency's principal, owner, or president: _____

   Length of time in business: _____ years

   Agency size: _____ employees

   Major clients: _____

   _____

   _____

   Area of specialization or agency focus: _____

   Source of your information (publication title and pages or Internet contact site and date):

   _____

   _____

   !!DO NOT PHONE THE AGENCY FOR THIS INFORMATION!!

The issue for debate is:

Should manufacturers of hard liquor be allowed to advertise on television?

1. **Background**

   Ten years ago, the alcohol industry agreed to pull its ads from the airwaves in a voluntary effort to appease opponents of drinking. However, beer and wine advertisers were allowed to continue on TV because the content of the beverages was under 10% alcohol.

   In late 1996, one advertiser decided to test the waters by advertising a Scotch liquor in a :30 commercial on network television. MADD was outraged, claiming that drinking is dangerous and harmful and should not be advertised. The alcohol industry claimed that the First Amendment allows free speech, and since the FTC has not ruled such advertising illegal, it will continue to broadcast its commercials. Absolut Vodka is also considering electronic media.

2. **Presenting your case**

   - Choose either the pro or the con side of this issue.

   - Research and present some facts to support your stance. [Newspaper editorials on the subject are available on NEXUS; reference advertising, then alcohol, then television.]

   - Type a one-page argument and include reference citations. Begin with: "Alcoholic beverages (should/should not) [choose one] be advertised on television because . . ."

1. Find an ad for a product that appears to use "puffery" to sell the product and attach it to this page. Answer the following questions about the ad, and be prepared to discuss it in class.

_____   _____   _____
Publication name   *Date*   *Product/service*

2. How could this product be sold without using puffery?

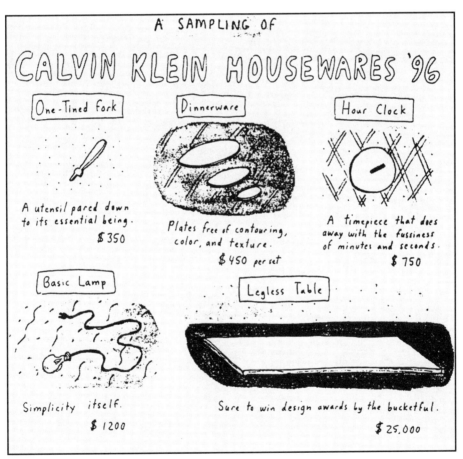

Drawing by R. Chast; © 1995 The New Yorker Magazine, Inc.

1. Study the following demographic data about movie goers in America:

Age	%M	%F	Income	%M	%F	Education	%M	%F
12–24	31	34	$25,000+	30	23	College Grad	45	39
25–34	35	31	$20–24,9000	16	15	HS Grad	35	43
35–49	15	17	$15–19,900	18	17	Nongrad	20	18
50–64	13	12	$10–14,900	18	22			
65+	06	06	Under $10K	18	23			

Decision to go to the movies in relationship to attendance:
- Same day   50%
- 1–2 weeks before   07%
- In past week   21%
- Over 2 weeks before   22%

Attends movies:
- With someone else   93% (51% with date or spouse)
                                    31% with friends
                                    11% with family
- Alone   07%

2. **Answer these questions:**

   a. What is the profile of the people most likely to attend a movie?

   b. If you wished to buy print advertising to reach movie goers, which medium would you buy? Why?

   c. What advertising appeals might you use?

Your client is going to sponsor a film festival on campus in April. Students from colleges across the nation are invited to submit their films for judging and showing during the three-day event. The client plans national publicity, media coverage, and public service advertising to promote the event. Consider the market and the four elements of the marketing mix—product, price, promotion, and place—to shape a strategy that can make this event a success. Use your text as a reference.

1. **The Market**
   a. What needs exist in the marketplace that this event is aimed at satisfying?

   b. What segment(s) of the population would you target for this event?

2. **Product**
   a. What qualities should the event have in order to be effective in satisfying the needs or desires of the chosen segment?

   b. What competitive position can you develop for this event—how can you set it apart from all the other film entertainment on or near campus?

©Hawaii International Film Festival.

3. **Price**
    a. What consideration must be given to price in order to market effectively to the chosen segment(s)?

    b. What costs are involved?

    c. What should be charged for admission?

    d. What attendance is required to reach a break-even point?

4. **Place**
    a. What distribution strategy should be used to sell tickets to the event?

    b. What campus and community locations may act as ticket outlets?

5. **Promotion**
    What promotional mix will be the most effective—will you use personal selling? advertising? publicity? sales promotion?

BUYING A MAGAZINE AD

You have been asked by your client, Golden Girl Jewelry, to select an advertising vehicle for its line of 14-karat gold earrings. GGJ wants to use full-page, four-color ads.

- Target Audience: Women 24–39 with household incomes of $40,000+, college graduates, living in major metro areas
- Product: Expensive, hand-crafted gold earrings
- Price: $400+ retail
- Place: Available at Neiman Marcus and specialty jewelry shops, U.S.

1. Your job is to select one publication for a three-insertion buy. Which of the following publications would you select? _____

2. Why is this the best choice? _____

3. What additional information would you need to make the most appropriate selection for your target audience? _____

Magazine	Readers per copy	Household income	Median age	% College grads	Circulation*	Rate** 4/c pg
Glamour	3.31	$33,000	28.2	42	2.00	$31.7
Vanity Fair	4.97	$42,500	31.7	48	.90	$24.6
Mademoiselle	3.66	$32,000	28.9	47	1.10	$23.3
New Yorker	5.12	$48,000	44.0	79	.48	$19.7
Vogue	5.27	$39,000	31.8	57	1.00	$25
Working Woman	2.89	$36,000	33.5	50	.70	$17.7

*Circulation is the rate base, expressed in millions.
**Rate is the one-time cost of a four-color page in thousands.

BUYING A NEWSPAPER AD

You want to place an ad 2 columns wide by 18 inches deep in a market with two newspapers with the following rates and readers:

Newspaper	Column-inch rate	Circulation
Post Herald	$37.50	208,680
Examiner	$31.50	172,550

1. What is the cost of each ad? (Multiply columns by inches; multiply total by rate.)

   a. Post Herald _____ b. Examiner _____

2. Which newspaper is more cost efficient?

   $$CPM = \frac{\text{Ad cost} \times 1000}{\text{circulation}}$$

   _____

Randy's Roudy Burgers advertises on radio stations with a variety of musical formats that appeal to adults 25–49. Randy asks you to consider one of three country western stations and advertise on the most cost efficient and the one that delivers the largest audience of the three stations in that format.

Station	:60 spot	Audience	Rating for Adults 25–49
KXXX	$150	47,000	1.5
KYYY	$300	74,000	2.4
KZZZ	$110	30,000	1.0

1. Calculate the CPM for each station.

   KXXX _____

   KYYY _____

   KZZZ _____

$$CPM = \frac{\text{Cost of Spot} \times 1000}{\text{Program's Audience}}$$

2. Calculate the CPRP for each station.

   KXXX _____

   KYYY _____

   KZZZ _____

$$CPM = \frac{\text{Cost of Commercial}}{\text{Program's Rating for Audience}}$$

3. Which is the most efficient station buy? _____

4. Which delivers the largest audience? _____

5. What other information do you need to make a station recommendation? _____

interviews

Part VII:
Expanding Your Horizons

book

evaluation

reports

preparation

questions

OUTSIDE ASSIGNMENT 1   An Informational Interview

To complete the Agency Visitation Report that follows, follow the steps discussed here.

Interviews provide you with the opportunity to ask questions about particular aspects of the business you cannot learn in class. For instance, you may talk with an art director to find out how he got his job, or with a media planner for an overview of her responsibilities. Choose an area that you are particularly interested in pursuing.

A. Research the options.

- Call your local advertising club for a list of local agencies, or consult the Yellow Pages.

- Find out as much as you can about the agency and its clients *before* you call for an appointment.

B. Call the agency.

- Ask the receptionist to schedule an appointment for an "informational interview" with a member of the agency. Make it clear that you are not job hunting and that this is a class assignment.

- Specify the position of the person you would like to see.

C. Prepare your questions.

- Use the knowledge you have about the agency to begin the interview, such as, "Your ads for XYZ client highlight the product's size. Why did you choose that strategy? What media do you suggest for that client?"

- Other questions to ask involve the individual's personal training (education, experience, travel) and how he or she became involved with advertising. How did they get their first job? Why did they choose this agency?

- Think up other questions and jot them down.

- Rehearse your questions.

D. Meet with your contact.

- Dress professionally.

- Take along a tape recorder instead of a notebook so you capture all the information.

E. Complete the Agency Visitation Report.

Agency Visitation Report

I, _____ ,

visited the _____ agency

located at _____

on _____. I met with _____

who is the agency's _____ .

This person's major clients are: _____

Describe your overall impressions, including ambiance, agency culture, etc.

Summarize what you learned about the advertising industry, the agency, and the person you interviewed, and explain how this interview influenced your attitudes about the advertising business.

OUTSIDE ASSIGNMENT 2   Book Report

A. Choose a book.

Select one of the books from the list on the next page or get permission from the instructor to select one of your own choosing.

The book I have selected is _____

B. Read the book.

C Complete the Book Report Form.

- The report is due on _____

Book Report Reading List

Bernbach, William, *A History of the Advertising that Changed the History of Advertising*, Villard, 1987.

Courtney, Alice and Thomas Whipple, *Sex Stereotyping in Advertising*, Lexington Books, 1983.

Coward, R., *Female Desires, How They Are Sought, Bought and Packaged*, Grove Press, 1985.

Davidson, M., *The Consumerist Manifesto: Advertising in Postmodern Times*, Routledge & Kegan-Paul, 1992.

Fjellman, Stephen, *Vinyl Leaves: Walt Disney World and America*, Westview Press, 1992.

Fowles, J., *Starstruck: Celebrity Performers and the American Public*, Smithsonian Institution Press, 1992.

Fox, Stephen, *The Mirror Makers: A History of American Advertising and its Creators*, Vintage Press, 1985.

Goodrum, Charles and Helen Dalrymple, *Advertising in America: The First 200 Years*, Harry Abrams Publishers, 1990.

Gossage, Howard, *Is There Any Hope for Advertising?* University of Illinois Press, 1986.

Jacobson, Michael and Louise Ann Mazior, *Marketing Madness*, Westview Press, 1995.

Kowinski, William, *The Malling of America: An Inside Look at the Great Consumer Paradise*, Morrow, 1985.

Lager, Fred, *Ben & Jerry's: The Inside Scoop*, Crown, 1994.

Lears, J., *Fables of Abundance: A Cultural History of Advertising in America*, Basic Books, 1994.

Lebergott, S., *Pursuing Happiness: American Consumers in the Twentieth Century*, Princeton University Press, 1993.

Lois, George, *What's the Big Idea?: How to Win with Outrageous Ideas that Sell*, Doubleday Currency, 1991.

Lyons, John, *Guts: Advertising from the Inside Out*, AMACON, 1987.

Maas, Jane, *Adventures of An Advertising Woman*, St. Martin's, 1986.

Marchand, Roland, *Advertising the American Dream*, University of California Press, 1985.

Mayer, M. *What Ever Happened to Madison Avenue?* Little, Brown, 1991.

Myers, William, *The Image Makers*, Times Books, 1984.

O'Barr, William, *Culture and the Ad: Exploring Otherness in the World of Advertising*, Westview Publishing, 1994.

Ogilvy, David, *Ogilvy on Advertising*, Vintage Press, 1985.

Ogilvy, David, *Confessions of an Advertising Man*, Atheneum, 1984.

Pope, Daniel, *The Making of Modern Advertising*, Basic Books, 1983.

Ritzer, George, *The McDonaldization of Society*, Pine Force Press, 1996.

Rotherberg, Randall, *Where the Suckers Moon*, Vintage Press, 1994.

Savan, Leslie, *The Sponsored Life*, Temple University Press, 1994.

Schudson, Michael, *Advertising, The Uneasy Persuasion*, Basic Books, 1984.

Sobieszek, Robert, *The Art of Persuasion: A History of Advertising Photography*, Abrams, 1988.

Stoltz, Donald, Marshall Stoltz, and William Earl, *The Advertising World of Norman Rockwell*, Madison Square Press, 1985.

This list is not complete, and you are welcome to select another book. However, if you choose a book not on this list, please check with the instructor before reading it.

Book Report Form

I, _____

read the book _____

by _____

    A. Summarize the main idea of the book in a paragraph.

    B. Describe a memorable incident or piece of advice that impressed you.

    C. Explain two concepts about advertising or marketing that you learned from reading this book.

Guest Lecture Evaluation Form

Visitor's name ——————————————— Title ———————————————

Company/Agency ——————————————————————————————

Circle the response that best describes your feelings about this presenter.
1. How *interesting* was the presenter?

   Not at all   Somewhat   Very interesting

2. How much did you *learn* that you did not know before?

   Nothing   A little bit   A great deal

3. How well did the presenter *convey the advertising experience* for you?

   Not at all   Somewhat   Very well

4. Would you recommend him/her to speak to another group of students?

   No way   Probably   Emphatically yes

In one or two sentences, summarize the message or lesson you received from this presenter.

If you have any strong feelings about the speaker, either positive or negative, please express them in the space provided. Your comments are useful for future speakers.

Your name ——————————————— Date ———————————————

Appendix: Student Ad Campaign Plan for NYNEX

On August 15, 1997, the new Bell Atlantic (NYSE:BEL) announced the merger of Bell Atlantic and NYNEX, following appproval by the Federal Communications Commission (FCC). The student ad campaign plan for NYNEX is reproduced with permission of Bell Atlantic and courtesy of students Sabrina Simon and Carrie S. Brooks.

AN ADVERTISING AGENCY

2300 Nutwood Ave. Fullerton, California 90623 (714) 555-1000

December 3, 1996

Mark Daleny
19089 Wilshire St.
Los Angeles, CA 90036

Dear Mr. Daleny:

APLUS Advertising is pleased to present to you the advertising campaign proposal for NYNEX. The enclosed advertising plan is geared towards the college market in Southern California. The plan covers all aspects of the campaign with research of the target market, media schedules, print and billboard ads. We hope that our plan will surpass all your expectations. Please feel free to contact us with any questions or comments. Thank you.

Sincerely,

A-Plus Advertising Agency

INTRODUCTION

Of the four major cellular companies in Southern California, AirTouch seemingly leads the market in cellular service. NYNEX, an international, multi-billion dollar company is setting its sights on the expanding Southern California college market. By promoting premium student rates and advertising directly to the college market, NYNEX plans to surpass its competitors by the year 2001. Using conventional media such as television, billboards, radio, and college newspapers, NYNEX seeks to launch a full-scale advertising campaign to increase sales in its target market.

By showcasing a reputable and dynamic image, NYNEX plans on setting its goals on becoming easily accessible to financially conscious students by promoting low college rates. Upon generating a high-quality image through superior service standards and advanced trendsetting technology, NYNEX invites everyone to . . .

RIDE THE CELLULAR WAVE!!

SITUATION ANALYSIS

NYNEX introduced its Cellular One mobile phone system into the New England market in 1987. At the time, Motorola dominated the market share at 45%, and Cellular One had a 30% share. A number of small firms shared the remaining 25% of the market. NYNEX rose to the top of the market using the AT&T and NYNEX logos, along with company marketing resources. Their huge expansion supported a West Coast venture.

The West Coast, however, proves to be a challenge for the company, as NYNEX has virtually no name recognition among cellular mobile services. So, the main obstacle is to gain awareness from our target market—the college students of Southern California.

NYNEX's competition in the cellular mobile service market includes Motorola, AirTouch, LA Cellular.

Strengths	Weaknesses
• Superior quality of service	• Low name recognition
• Extensive benefits, such as paging and voice mail	• Competition of brands offering similar choices
• Special rates for college students	• Limited resources of the target market
• Free trail period for qualified college students	

MARKETING MIX

Product

NYNEX, a global corporation specializing in customer satisfaction, technical advances, and communications networking, positioned itself as an international leader in cellular service. NYNEX has introduced a number of new developments by merging with Bell Atlantic, making it the largest communications network on the East Coast. NYNEX has a vast array of products, telecommunications systems, and technology available to its customers.

Price

Due to NYNEX's introduction to the West Coast, it has available to its college customers a wide variety of discounts and plans from which to pick and choose. A free trial service is offered for the first 30 days to prospective customers and special college student discounts are given to those choosing or switching to NYNEX.

Place

NYNEX is established on the East Coast and is introducing itself to the Southern California marketplace. With its merger with Bell Atlantic, it is now a global corporation able to offer its services worldwide. NYNEX has the advantage of years of service and large communications networks, with which to meet the demand for cellular service on the West Coast.

MARKET PLAN OBJECTIVES

Our marketing objective is to increase cellular use by college students, ages 18-26. NYNEX, a newly established company on the West Coast, must first create awareness among the college segment in order to meet its marketing objectives. Our main objective is to break down current perceptions of cellular service and reinforce reliability, convenience, and affordability.

NYNEX would like to increase its market share by 15 percent and its target market share by 30 percent during the first year.

Direct Action

This objective promotes NYNEX's cost-efficient rates and wide range of services for students. We will create awareness with non-cellular users as well as persuade non-NYNEX users to switch by offering student discounts and free cellular phones to sample. Following the period of free trial, new users will be encouraged to continue using the service at a reduced student rate.

Modify Attitudes

Preliminary research shows that students find it difficult to justify the purchase of a cellular phone on a limited budget. In an attempt to change this perception, NYNEX will offer a 30-day trial with ten hours of free phone usage. With no cost to the student, we will have succeeded in our effort to change the image of inaccessibility to the college student.

Reinforce Attitudes

Once the students have access to full-time cellular phone usage, they will have had an opportunity to experience its convenience and usefulness. Following the free trial period, the student will be encouraged to sign on for a more extensive contract with reduced student rates. Informal agency surveys of cellular users revealed that a "free" offer enticed them into signing on with a long-term contract. Additionally, NYNEX is known for its exceptional customer service, which will be promoted at the point-of-sale.

Budget Method

Share-of-Market: The budget plan used will accommodate the specific objective designed to create an awareness among college students. Having an unlimited budget will enable us to compete and exceed prior competitive budgets.

CUSTOMER CHARACTERISTICS

Demographically

Age:	18-25
Education:	currently attending college
Occupation:	student and/or part-time employment
Marital status:	single
Household:	varies
Residence:	renter, dorm occupant, living with parents
Socioeconomic:	lower-middle to upper

Psychographically

College students who are goal-oriented, driven, and ambitious. Students who are open-minded and more accepting and tolerant of change. Young, single people with limited financial freedom and very budgeted time. Also very outgoing.

Behaviors

- Socially active
- Not easily persuaded
- Noncommittal
- Practical
- Trendsetters

PRIMARY RESEARCH REPORT

The agency conducted primary research to determine awareness levels of college students regarding NYNEX. Using convenience sample, 54 students, ages 18-25, completed surveys the second week of October 1996; 64% were females, and 36% were males. There were 2 freshmen, 6 sophomores, 30 juniors, and 16 seniors.

Survey Results

Top of mind awareness was greatest for Motorola, as it was mentioned first by 34 students. LA Cellular was the next popular with 11 votes. AirTouch came in a close third being mentioned 9 times. Other brands mentioned were Sony, Toshiba, NEC, and Nokia. NYNEX was not represented by any responses.

Research shows that while most college students felt that cell phones are expensive, they also believe them to be very convenient and useful. Female students surveyed found them to be more necessary that the male students.

The general consensus of the survey group was that they would be most likely to use a cellular phone in the case of an emergency so that they could be reached. Other situations mentioned were calling for a tow truck and calling for directions if lost.

The majority of cellular phone usage is for business purposes; however, emergency use is another factor. Students, especially women, are concerned for their safety, but their budgets do not afford them all the tools for ensuring complete security. A free cellular phone as well as special student rates would be effective promotional tools in convincing students to make a purchase that they would not ordinarily make because of the expense.

Students were asked how likely they were to use a mobile service in the next six months. Surprisingly, the responses were split in half. Fifty percent of the students said they were likely to use the service, and the other half said they were unlikely. Again, most of the likely responses were that of the female subjects. All of the students said that they would take into consideration the company from which they were purchasing service before doing so.

Implications for Advertising

According to our survey, NYNEX has great potential and opportunity to gain in market share and awareness among college students. Promotions can be geared around special student rates and free phones since students have limited financial resources. On-campus sites for trying the phones can take advantage of students' spontaneity and open minds.

Top of Mind Awareness
of Cellular Services

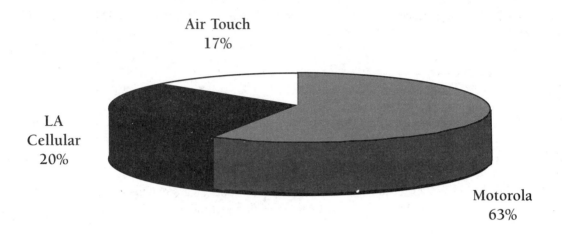

Air Touch
17%

LA
Cellular
20%

Motorola
63%

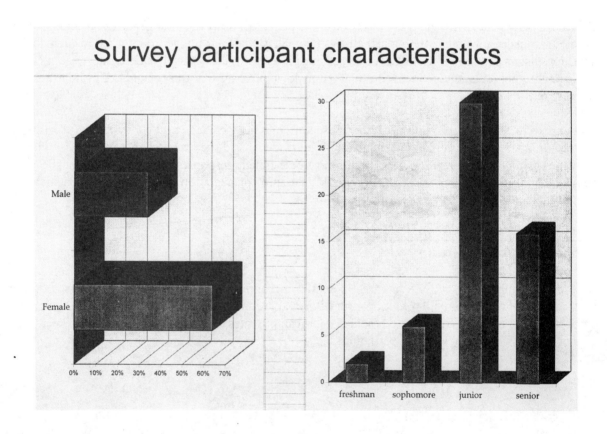

Survey participant characteristics

Male

Female

0% 10% 20% 30% 40% 50% 60% 70%

30

25

20

15

10

5

0

freshman   sophomore   junior   senior

MEDIA PLAN

Our goal is to target the commuting student of Southern California, which in itself is a challenge. Campaign media vehicles will be television, radio, print, and billboards. The media for this campaign will be chosen based on ratings for audiences with an age range of 18-26. The campaign will run from January 1997 through November 1997, with decreased media programming during off-semester periods.

Television

We will attempt to reach the maximum number of our target audience with spot ads run on cable television stations such as MTV and ESPN with local rates. This will give us a better CPM by reaching our target market in each location. We will include spots on Fox television shows such as "Melrose Place," which airs Monday nights, with a package to include a spot on Wednesday nights during "Party of Five." These shows run during Prime Time slots but have high ratings among our target market.

Print

Ads will be placed in college newspapers in the region. Though readership is fairly low on commuter college campuses, you are sure to reach almost total target market audience. Ads will also be placed in fall, winter, and spring issues of *Details*, *Cosmopolitan*, and *Surfing* magazines.

- *Details* is based in Southern California and has a high readership of our target audience, both male and female.
- *Cosmopolitan* will reach the females in our target market.
- *Surfing* magazine will be reaching the males in our target audience.

Radio

Radio ads will correspond with the television campaign. Spots will be aired on stations that reach our target market during peak commuting hours. The stations chosen are KROQ (106.7-FM), KSTR (98.7-FM), KPWR (105.9-FM), and KIIS (102.7-FM).

Billboards

Billboards will be placed at local freeways near targeted college campuses during school semesters. Your target audience takes these routes frequently on the commute to their respective universities. Most importantly we will reach a large audience at relatively low cost.

NYNEX MEDIA SCHEDULE

Campaign Starts January 1997; ends November 1997

	January	February	March	April	May	June	July	August	September	October	November
PRINT											
College Newspapers/Magazines											
• Full-page B/W newspaper ads alternating Tuesday and Thursday one week; and Wednesday and Friday the next week. Ads in Details, Surfing and Cosmopolitan magazines. All print during school sessions only.											
BROADCAST											
Radio											
• :30 second spots KROQ, KIIS, STAR, and Power 106 Monday-Friday 6:00-10:00 am and 3:00-7:00 pm											
TELEVISION											
• :30 second spots ESPN, MTV and FOX Monday-Wednesday 8:00 pm to Midnight ESPN and MTV Saturday and Sunday Noon to 6:00 pm											
OUTDOOR											
Billboard/Marquee											

PRINT ADS
College Papers, Details, Cosmopolitan Surfing

CABLE TV
ESPN: Sports Center
MTV: Singled Out

NETWORK TV
Melrose Place Mon.
90210, Party of Five   Wed.

BILLBOARDS
Southern California college campus freeway ramp locations.

NYNEX Media Campaign Budget

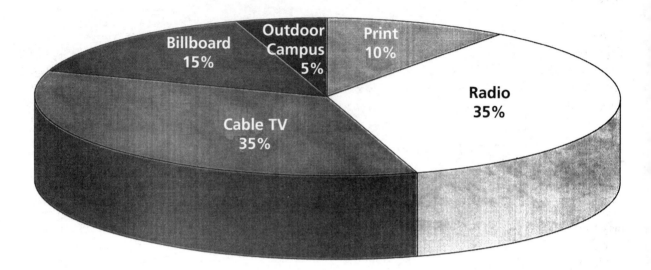

CREATIVE TEAM STRATEGY

Intended Goal

Introducing NYNEX, an East Coast-based company, into the Southern California college market. Concentrating on the college segment, the campaign intends to break down the current social images of expensive, impractical, and high-status usage of cellular phones. By promoting cost efficient student rates and outstanding service through radio, television, and billboard media, the campaign expects to become a top-of-mind name among cellular users and non-users.

Strategy

By dividing the strategy into three stages of awareness, promotion, and brand recognition, we are able to introduce NYNEX as a healthy competitor in the cellular market. Each individual stage represents the task to be accomplished. The stages will introduce the NYNEX name to the college segment, promote student rates, and reinstate brand awareness, respectively. Humor and images of sunny Southern California are used in the campaign in the hope of creating a fun, exciting, and inexpensive alternative to existing competition.

Awareness

This stage introduces the NYNEX company to the market as the "new kid on the block" by highlighting the expansion to the West Coast. Two character spokespeople are used to represent the bi-coastal transfer. Frankie, a Southern California surfer dude, and Rita, a New Yorker, help illustrate the move of NYNEX to the Southern California market. The radio/television ads contain dialogue between Frankie and Rita comparing the advantages of living on each side of the U.S. The spot ends with Rita bragging that New York has NYNEX. The snappy comeback from Frankie corrects her and adds that now NYNEX is also in Southern California.

Promotion

This stage identifies the promotional student rates offered by NYNEX to its college market. All chosen media vehicles are used. Frankie and Rita are also used again to illustrate announcement of exciting news for college students.

Recognition

This stage, in a sense, wraps the whole campaign together. By identifying NYNEX with its logo and catchy slogan—*"Riding the Cellular Wave"*—NYNEX hopes to become a top-of-mind name brand and surpass the already established names of other services.

NYNEX
IS COMING. . . ,
DUDE.

NYNEX RIDING THE CELLULAR WAVE

For more info: 1-800-GO-NYNEX

Ny•nex (ni'neks), *n.*

1. intrigue; new. 2. coming to Southern California. 3. looking to help college students live easier and safer. 4. necessary; inexpensive.

1-800-GO-NYNEX

Ever ridden a cellular wave??

NYNEX RIDING THE CELLULAR WAVE

A-Plus

RADIO SCRIPT

CLIENT: NYNEX   DATE: 12/4

PRODUCT: CELLULAR SERVICE   LENGTH: :30

TITLE: COAST TO COAST

CHARACTERS: RITA: TYPICAL NEW YORKER ACCENT, COCKY ATTITUDE.
                FRANKIE: SURFER ACCENT, HUMOROUS OUTLOOK ON LIFE.

INTRO—Music to "New York, New York"

Rita	Hey, Southern California. New York has everything! We've got the Empire State Building, the Statue of Liberty, and the Yankees just won the World Series!
Frankie	Whoa, lady! One problem, though, you can't surf in New York!
Rita	So what. We've got Manhattan.
Frankie	We'll we've got Manhattan Beach.
Rita	We've got Long Island, too!
Frankie	And we've got Long Island Ice Teas!

MUSIC SLOWLY FADES TO SILENCE

Rita	We'll we've got NYNEX cellular service, the best on the east coast, baby!
Frankie	Dude . . . no anymore 'cause NYNEX is coming to Southern California!

MUSIC TO "SURF CITY" FADE IN

AVO	NYNEX: Riding the Cellular Wave

A-Plus

RADIO SCRIPT #2

CLIENT: NYNEX

PRODUCT: CELLULAR SERVICE

TITLE: STUDENT RATES

INTRO: Beach Boys tune playing softly in background

SFX: Phone ringing

Frankie:	Hello?
Rita:	Frankie? It's Rita. What's this I hear about NYNEX giving special deals to college students out there?
Frankie:	Yeah, it's bitchin'! NYNEX is giving free phones, free startup, and half-price rates, plus free weekend calling to full-time college students only in Southern Cal!!
Rita:	We never got student discounts here in New York!
Frankie:	I know. Isn't it sweet? All I have to do is show up for my Ecology Awareness classes and I can talk all weekend . . . For free!!
Rita:	You Southern Californians. You get all the breaks!
Frankie:	That's right . . . and I'm gonna catch one right now!!

SFX: Waves crashing with distant "Cowabunga!" call fading in.

VO: "NYNEX, Riding the Cellular Wave."

A-Plus

RADIO SCRIPT #3

CLIENT: NYNEX

PRODUCT: CELLULAR SERVICE

TITLE: STILL RIDING THE CELL WAVE

SFX:	Ocean waves crashing
SFX:	Phone ringing
VO:	"Whoa . . . NYNEX, still riding the cellular wave!"

SALES PROMOTION

Our target market is Southern California college-age students. This particular group tends to have limited income resources and research shows that a cellular phone is not a desired necessity in their lives at this time.

Through promotions, NYNEX will raise the level of desire to use cellular phones in the mind of the student by making it affordable.

NYNEX will set up promotion stands at all Southern California college campuses. A press release will announce reduced student rates. Qualified students will have the opportunity to sample a NYNEX cellular phone with ten hours of free service.

NYNEX

5334 Ketch   Simi Valley, California 95542   (800) 224-CELL

Free Phones for College Students

For Immediate Release:
December 4, 1996

Contact: Anita Mignosa
(714) 848-8520

Boston—Nov. 27, 1996—NYNEX, a leading cellular service provider in New England, today announced a unique promotion giving free cellular phones with paging capabilities and free air time to Southern California college students. NYNEX representatives will be visiting major universities from January until November of 1997, to promote their service.

"NYNEX offers the most advanced personal communication device available. With cellular and paging capabilities combined in one unit plus ten free hours of usage, we are helping to make the student's life safer and less hectic," said Rebecca Jones, Promotions Manager for NYNEX.

Representatives will be on campus to sign up students for their 10 free hours under no obligation. When the 10 hours have been used, the holder may keep the phone and sign a Student Discount Contract or simply return the phone to NYNEX.

Those who sign the Student Discount Contract will receive the first six months at 50 percent off along with free weekends, five hours of free emergency calls, and ten hours blocked time at a rate of ten cents a minute. The block will be a unique set which the student creates. If the student wants the phone with no blocking or specials, they may still get the five hours of emergency calling. Student customers will pay a base rate of ten dollars a month.

In 1987, NYNEX introduced Cellular One mobile system into the New England market. In 1995, the company generated $14.31 million. NYNEX currently has 35% of the market share in California. They have over 500 service offices in four California regions.

Using AT&T technology, NYNEX offers the most advanced cellular service available for clarity and reliability. For more information on NYNEX Cellular Mobile Service, please contact NYNEX Sales at (800) 224-CELL or (818) 554-0369, (818) 554-0370 (fax) or by e-mail ussales @NYNEX.com.